The EVERYDAY JOURNEYS of ORDINARY THINGS

From Phones to Food and From Post to Poo... The Ways the World Works

Libby Deutsch

illustrated by Valpuri Kerttula

IVY KIDS

CONTENTS

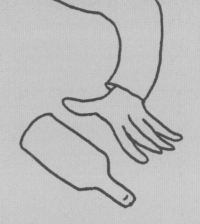

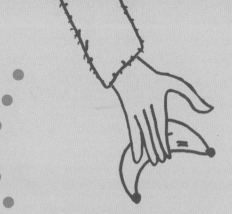

IMAGINE...

It's Saturday morning. You switch on the bathroom light, go to the toilet and stand under the shower, humming along to your favourite song on the radio. Then you pull on your jeans and run downstairs for breakfast. The newspaper comes through the letterbox as you pour milk over a big bowl of cereal, slice up a banana and switch on the TV to watch your favourite show.

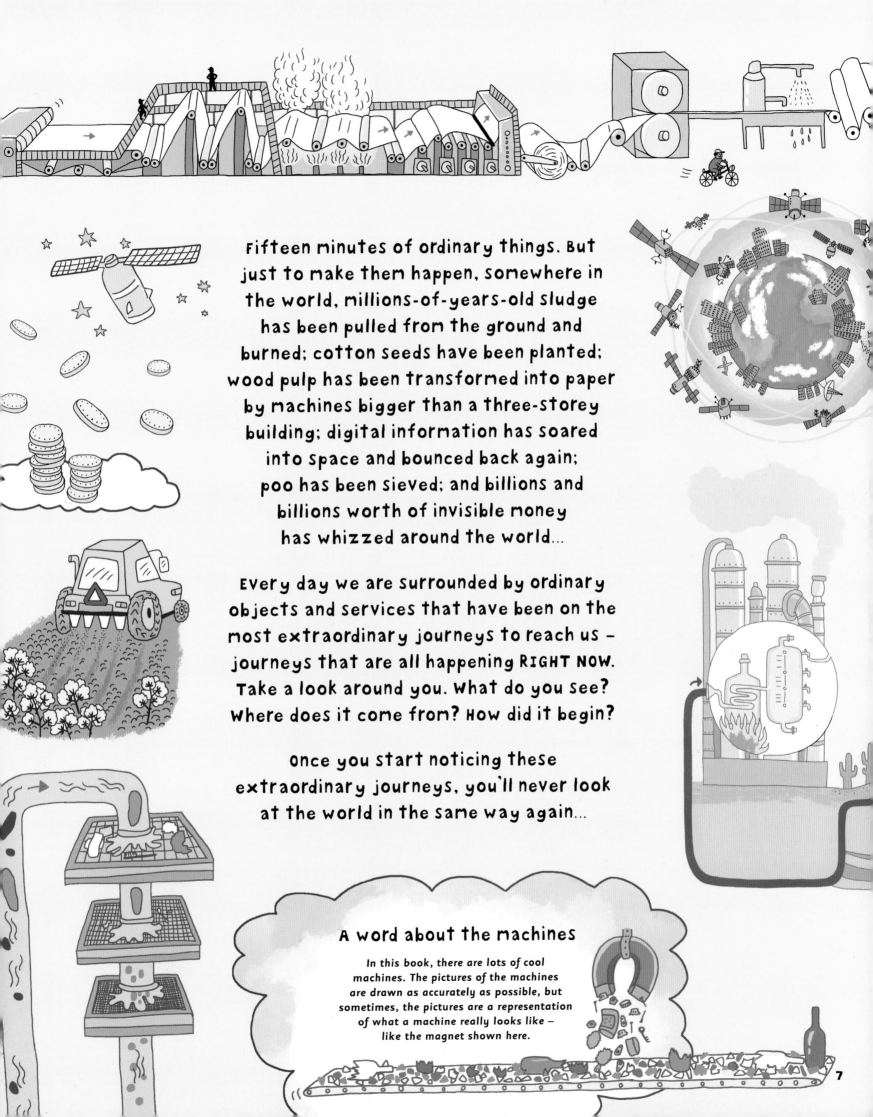

Fifteen minutes of ordinary things. But just to make them happen, somewhere in the world, millions-of-years-old sludge has been pulled from the ground and burned; cotton seeds have been planted; wood pulp has been transformed into paper by machines bigger than a three-storey building; digital information has soared into space and bounced back again; poo has been sieved; and billions and billions worth of invisible money has whizzed around the world...

Every day we are surrounded by ordinary objects and services that have been on the most extraordinary journeys to reach us – journeys that are all happening RIGHT NOW. Take a look around you. What do you see? Where does it come from? How did it begin?

Once you start noticing these extraordinary journeys, you'll never look at the world in the same way again...

A word about the machines

In this book, there are lots of cool machines. The pictures of the machines are drawn as accurately as possible, but sometimes, the pictures are a representation of what a machine really looks like – like the magnet shown here.

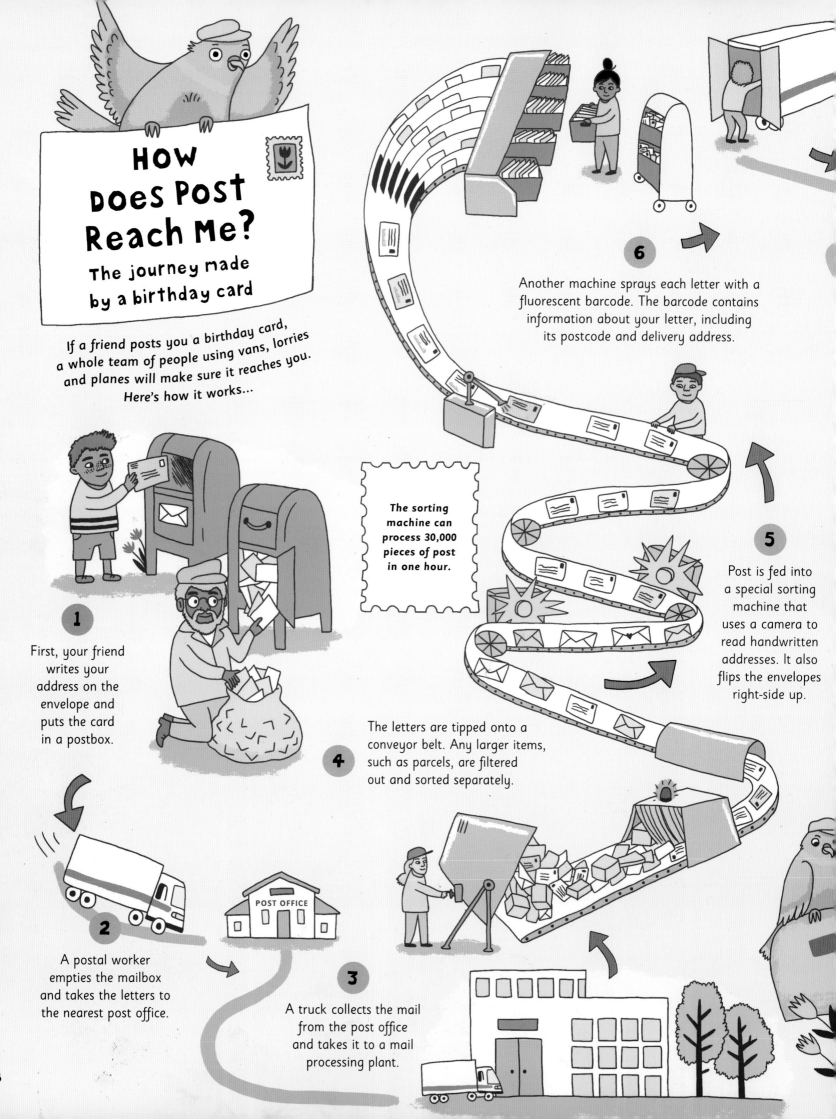

HOW DOES POST Reach Me?

The journey made by a birthday card

If a friend posts you a birthday card, a whole team of people using vans, lorries and planes will make sure it reaches you. Here's how it works...

1 First, your friend writes your address on the envelope and puts the card in a postbox.

2 A postal worker empties the mailbox and takes the letters to the nearest post office.

3 A truck collects the mail from the post office and takes it to a mail processing plant.

4 The letters are tipped onto a conveyor belt. Any larger items, such as parcels, are filtered out and sorted separately.

The sorting machine can process 30,000 pieces of post in one hour.

5 Post is fed into a special sorting machine that uses a camera to read handwritten addresses. It also flips the envelopes right-side up.

6 Another machine sprays each letter with a fluorescent barcode. The barcode contains information about your letter, including its postcode and delivery address.

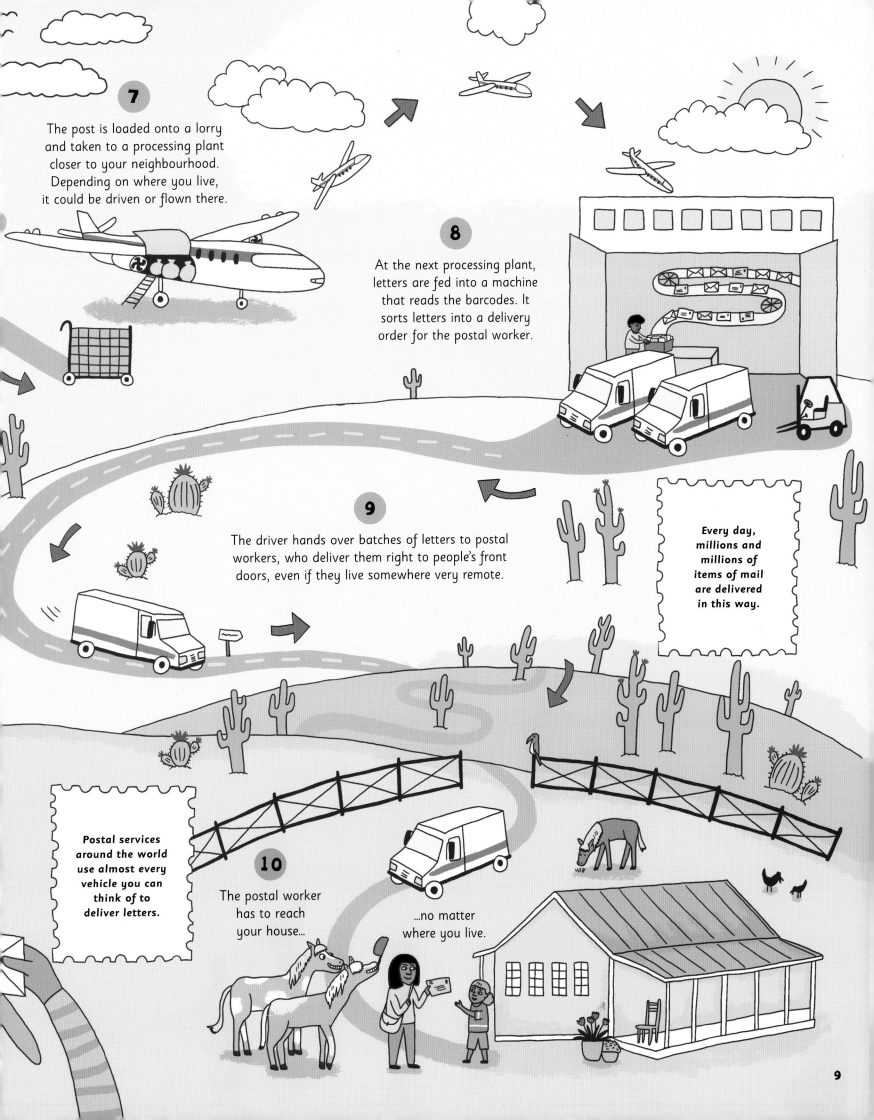

7

The post is loaded onto a lorry and taken to a processing plant closer to your neighbourhood. Depending on where you live, it could be driven or flown there.

8

At the next processing plant, letters are fed into a machine that reads the barcodes. It sorts letters into a delivery order for the postal worker.

9

The driver hands over batches of letters to postal workers, who deliver them right to people's front doors, even if they live somewhere very remote.

Every day, millions and millions of items of mail are delivered in this way.

Postal services around the world use almost every vehicle you can think of to deliver letters.

10

The postal worker has to reach your house...

...no matter where you live.

Does Food Grow on Shelves?

The journey of a banana

It's so easy to go down to the shop and pick up almost anything you need off the shelves. But where does it all come from? The answer is: all over the world. Let's take a look at the journey made by one of our favourite foods – bananas.

1 Bananas come mostly from countries around the Equator. These have a tropical climate where it's warm all year round, with lots of rain.

Each large cluster of bananas is called a 'banana stem'. One stem is made up of several tiers (or levels) of bunches of bananas. The correct name for a bunch of bananas is a 'hand', and a single banana is known as a 'finger'.

2 Bananas grow on a farm for crops called a plantation. They grow in big, heavy bunches. Farmers hang plastic bags around the bananas while they are growing to protect them from wasps and birds.

3 Bananas are harvested when they have grown to a certain size but are still green. People don't like buying bruised bananas, so the fruit must be handled with great care. Foam pads are placed between the bunches to protect them.

4 The workers carry the stems from the tree and hang them on a trolley rail. When all the stems have been harvested, workers pull them along the rail to the sorting depot.

7

Each 'hand' of bananas is stickered with the label of the plantation it comes from, packed carefully into boxes and taken by a lorry to the port.

8

At the port, the boxes of bananas are packed on refrigerated ships called 'reefers'. They have carefully controlled airflow and temperature to keep the fruit cool so that it doesn't ripen while it is being transported.

6

Each 'hand' of bananas is then cut from the main stem, put into water to protect the fruit and checked again for quality. Any bruised bananas are removed and sold cheaply at local markets.

Depending upon the route, a reefer ship usually takes between 4 to 12 days to reach its destination. Some ships are built to keep the fruit fresh for as long as 50 days.

9

Once the bananas arrive at their destination, the fruit is stored in a large warehouse filled with moist, warm air that helps the bananas begin to ripen again.

5

At the depot, the bananas are checked carefully again for size and quality. Then they are washed and sprayed with fungicide to keep them free from diseases.

10

When the bananas are perfectly ripe, they are loaded on to lorries and taken to shops, ready to be bought by you!

Where on Earth Are You?

The journey of GPS

Wherever you are, satellite navigation systems can locate you. But how does that information reach you when you might be up a mountain, trekking through a desert or sailing on the vast ocean?

1

Yes! You're going to see your favourite band, Which Direction?, with your best friend. Your gran is taking you both, but she doesn't know exactly where the venue is — or even exactly where you are! She takes out her smartphone and goes to her navigation app.

2

Meanwhile, approximately 27 satellites are orbiting Earth, each equipped with an onboard computer, radio transmitter and very precise atomic clock. They continuously transmit information about their exact location and time via radio waves. These waves are travelling towards Earth at the speed of light. Together, the satellites form the Global Positioning System, or GPS.

Each satellite follows a route, travelling around Earth twice a day. Their routes are set so that there are always at least three satellites within range of your phone. They transmit a list of where they should be and when — like a bus timetable!

GPS satellites are not the only objects orbiting Earth. There are hundreds of thousands of pieces of space rubbish, including a spanner and an astronaut's glove!

8

You have arrived. Your gran switches off the navigation app on her phone. When the concert is over, she can use it to find the way home again. Have fun!

PRESENTS
WHICH DIRECTION?

7

Suddenly, the navigation app on your gran's phone starts to work! The control station's broadcasts have reached it. Her receiver is also picking up information from a fourth satellite, so it gives a more accurate reading.

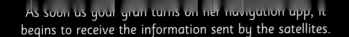

As soon as your gran turns on her navigation app, it begins to receive the information sent by the satellites.

- Each satellite transmits its precise location and the exact time to the nearest nanosecond.
- The receiver on the phone subtracts the time that the information was transmitted from the time it was received.
- Knowing that the information travelled at the speed of light, your receiver can tell your distance from the satellite.

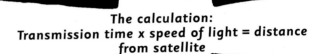

The calculation:
Transmission time x speed of light = distance from satellite

4

Knowing how far you are from one satellite doesn't tell you where you are. But your gran's receiver is getting this information from three different satellites. A point in each of the three readings will be the same – that's where your gran's phone is.

5

Hmm, something's not working on your gran's app. It keeps showing her she is somewhere else. This is because some of the signals the phone is picking up have been delayed. Firstly, they were slowed down by the electromagnetic field surrounding Earth, and also the bad weather. Because they can't travel through solid objects like the tall buildings around you, they are taking a while to get through. The app doesn't know this though. It makes its calculations assuming that the signal travelled to you at the speed of light.

6

A local control station has picked up that the transmissions from one satellite are getting delayed. The control station is in a fixed position and has the list that says where each satellite should be and when. So it can tell when a transmission from a satellite is inaccurate. The control station recalculates the satellite's information and rebroadcasts it to the surrounding area.

The satellites are solar powered, and usually last for about ten years. When they are replaced, the new model will have new features and the latest technology onboard.

Where do clothes come from?

The journey of a pair of jeans

Jeans as we know them today were created by Levi Strauss in 1850 and have been made in a similar way ever since. Let's see how!

Jeans are made from a fabric called denim, a stiff cotton material. This was originally produced in France, in a town called Nîmes. In French, 'from Nîmes' is 'de Nîmes' – or 'denim'!

1

Do jeans grow on trees? Well... yes, or at least on plants. Cotton seeds are planted by farmers in spring, and grow into bushy, 1-metre-high plants. By late summer, the clumps of cotton, or bolls, are ready to be picked. They look a lot like the cotton wool that you buy in a shop. The bolls are sold at a cotton market, and taken to the jeans factory to be processed.

2

At the factory, the raw cotton is put through a carding machine. Cards are wire-toothed brushes that clean, untangle and straighten the cotton fibres. After carding, the cotton is left in straight tufts called slivers.

CARDING MACHINE

CLOSE-UP OF CARDING MACHINE

3

The slivers are stretched, pulled and twisted together many times on a spinning machine to make long lines of thread. These are wound onto giant spools.

SPINNING MACHINE

Unlike most cloth, which is woven first and then dyed, most denim is dipped in an indigo dye before the thread is woven.

4

Now the white cotton thread is dyed. The most common colour for denim is blue, so a dye called indigo is used. Every factory has its own secret method. The number of dips, the length of each dip and the time in between dips all help create exactly the shade the manufacturer wants.

5

After dyeing, the thread is coated in starch to make it stiffer and stronger. Then machines weave the thread into cloth. The warp (lengthways thread) is blue. The weft (crossways thread) is white. On denim, the warp is woven more tightly than the weft, which is why the overall appearance of the fabric is blue. You can see the white weft threads hanging down on frayed jeans.

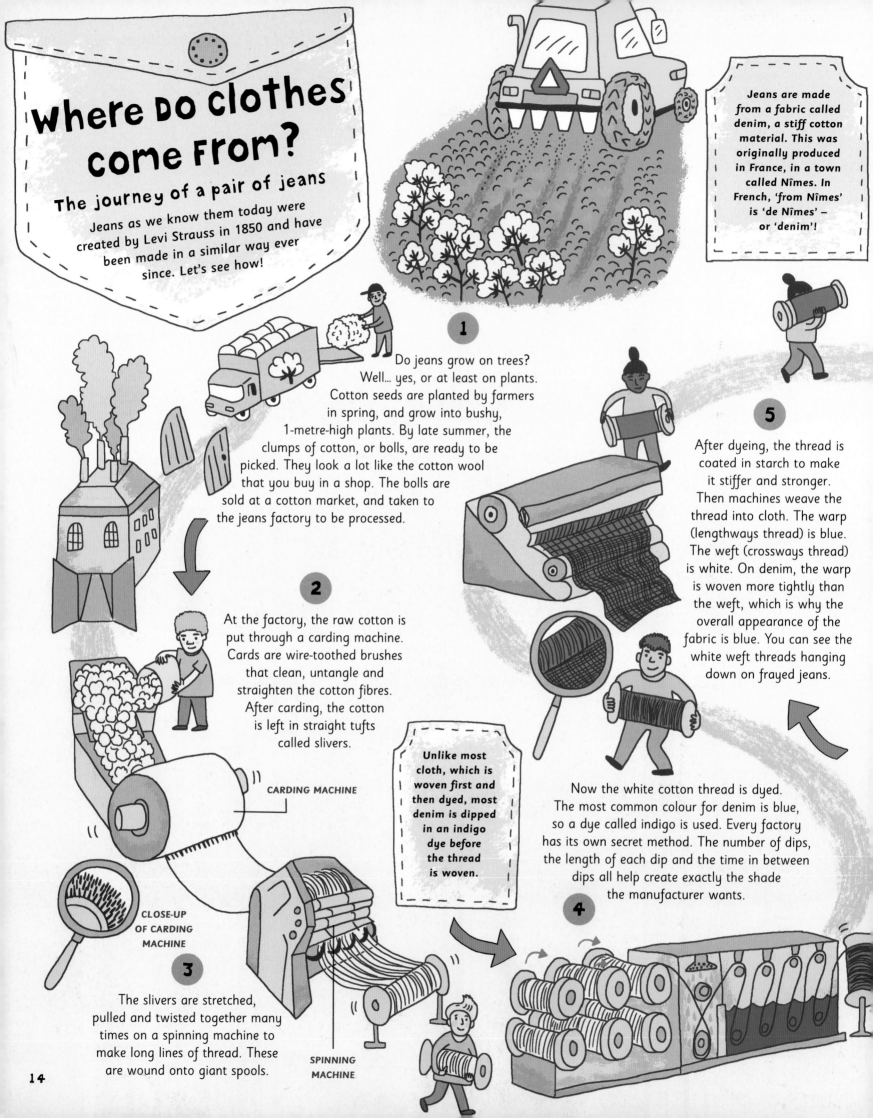

An average jeans factory can make about 2,500 pairs of jeans every day.

7

Pattern cutters cut the cloth using a machine. They wear a chainmail glove so that they don't risk cutting their hand.

8

Once the pieces are cut, people sew them together on an assembly line. Each person has one specific job to complete before passing the garment on to the next person.

- Pockets sewn onto back
- Leg pieces sewn together
- Waistband attached
- Belt loops stitched on
- Buttons or zipper attached
- Bottom of legs hemmed
- Rivets punched in and maker's label stitched on.

6

Now the pattern for the jeans is drawn out onto paper. This is laid on top of the denim, which is stacked into layers of up to 100 and held down by heavy weights.

It takes around 15 separate pieces to make up a pair of standard jeans.

9

The jeans are finished, but it's fashionable for jeans to look faded and well-worn, even when they are brand new.

Sometimes the jeans are frayed by hand with sandpaper or a razor, and sometimes they are deliberately ripped.

The more 'treatments' jeans are given to damage them, the more expensive they are!

The jeans may be sprayed with bleach, to give them a faded appearance.

Jeans may be sandblasted – sprayed with gritty sand to wear away the fabric in some places.

Sometimes the jeans are stonewashed. This involves putting them in giant washing machines with lots of rough stones for up to six hours.

10

Finally, the jeans are checked for quality, packed and taken by a lorry to shops and online retailer warehouses, ready for you to buy them.

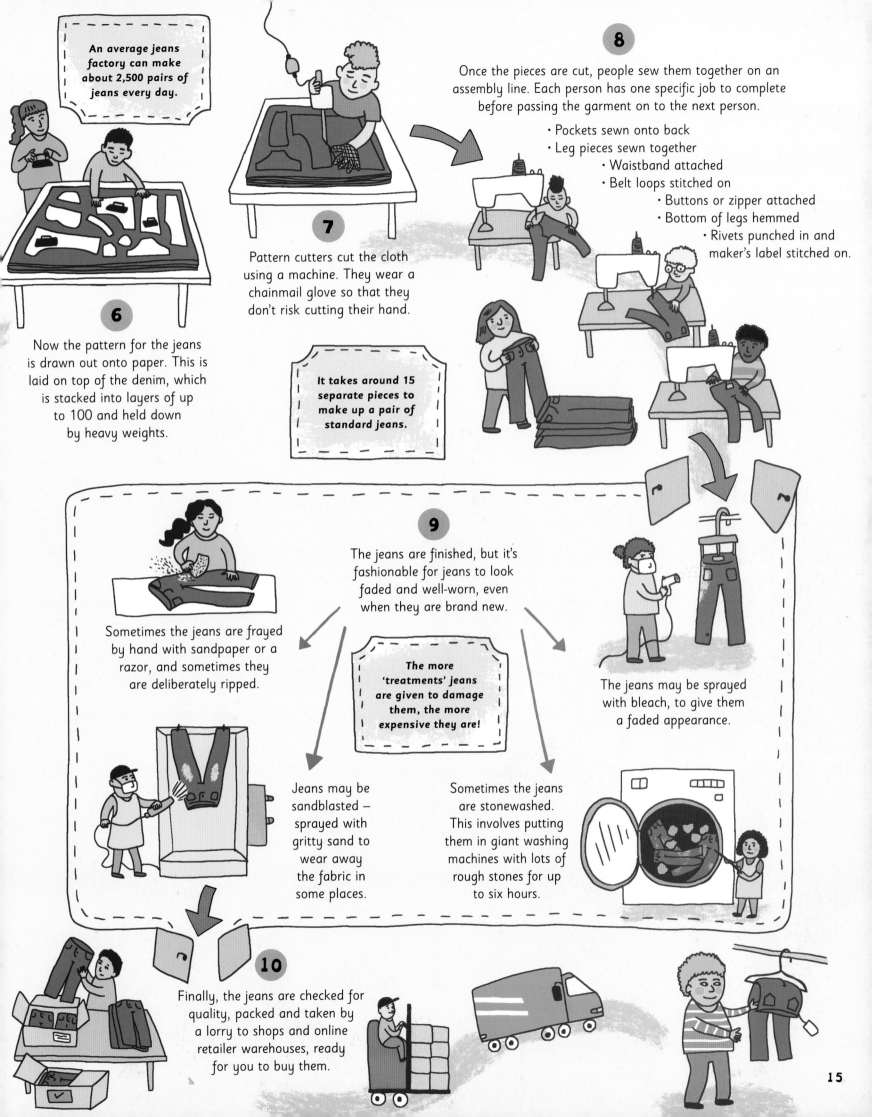

15

From Tree to Paper
The journey of paper

This piece of paper you're reading right now used to be a tree. Hard to imagine, isn't it? So how exactly does hard, bumpy wood become smooth, wafer-thin paper? Let's see...

Some trees are taken from a renewable source – a plantation where new trees are grown to replace those that are cut down.

1 First, the trees are logged – cut down and piled up. They are taken to a factory called a paper mill.

7 The pulp is sprayed out onto a wire mesh. Huge rollers press the pulp many times over, squeezing out as much water as possible.

6 The pulp is mixed with water and fillers such as clay. These will fill in any lumps in the wood fibres, giving the final paper a smooth appearance. Bleach is added again to make the paper whiter.

CLAY

WATER

This is actually one huge machine.

8 As it is rolled and pressed, the fibres web together and form a single continuous sheet.

Paper-making machines are huge: almost four times the length of an Olympic-sized swimming pool and as tall as a three-storey building.

9 The paper is carried across the longest part of the paper-making machine: the drying cylinders. These blow air out at 100°C, drying and strengthening the paper as it passes over each one.

The paper sheet passes through the paper-making machine at up to 1,400 metres per minute.

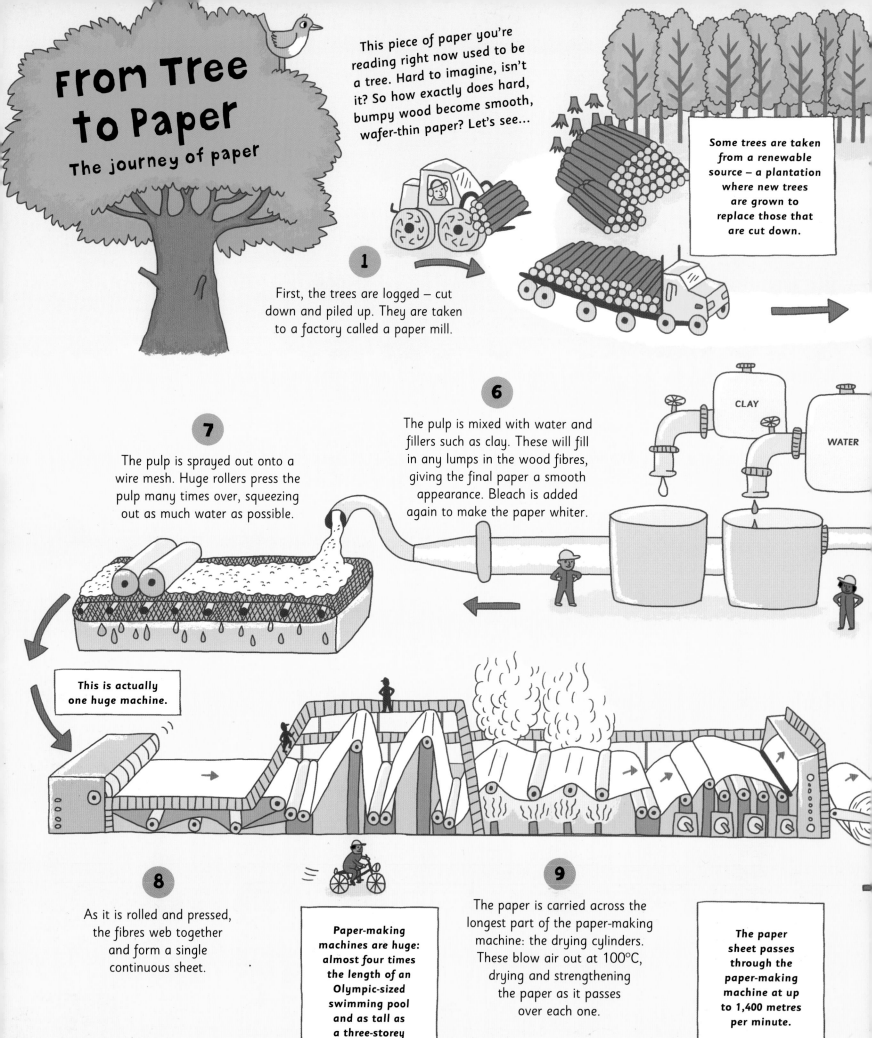

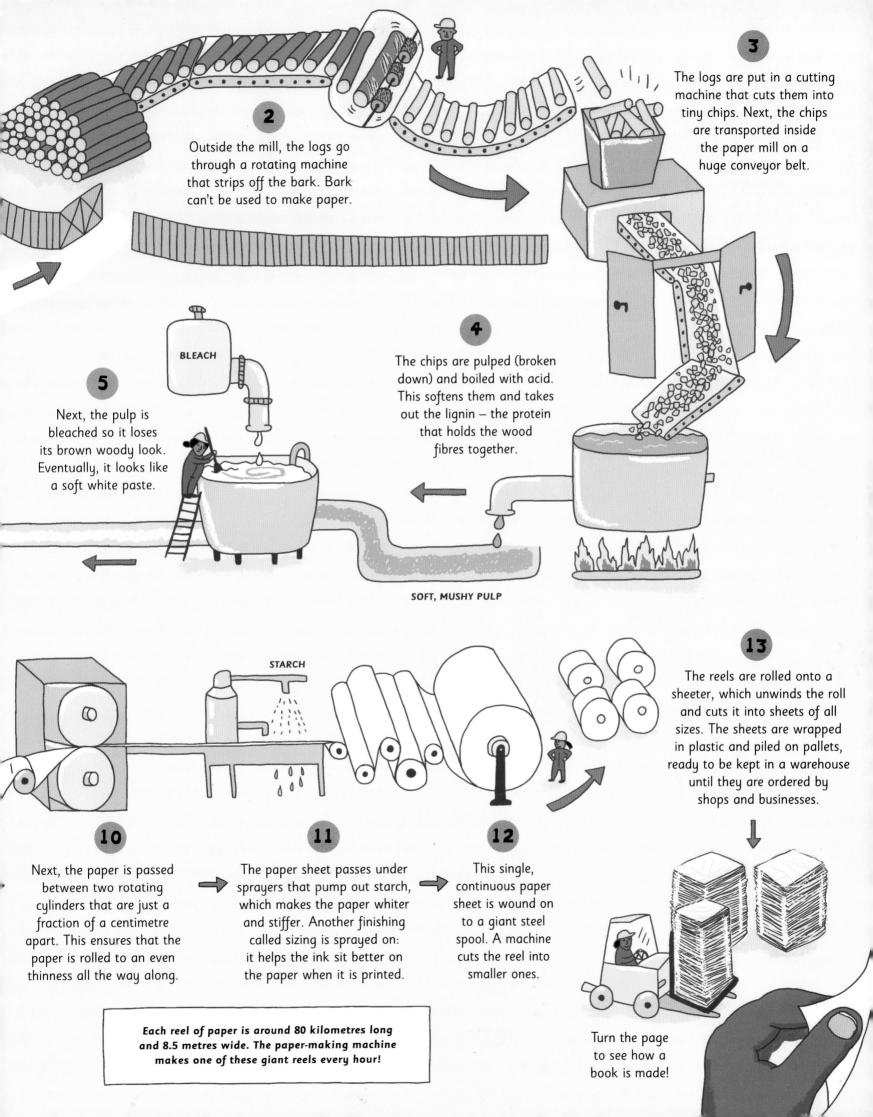

2

Outside the mill, the logs go through a rotating machine that strips off the bark. Bark can't be used to make paper.

3

The logs are put in a cutting machine that cuts them into tiny chips. Next, the chips are transported inside the paper mill on a huge conveyor belt.

4

The chips are pulped (broken down) and boiled with acid. This softens them and takes out the lignin – the protein that holds the wood fibres together.

5

Next, the pulp is bleached so it loses its brown woody look. Eventually, it looks like a soft white paste.

BLEACH

SOFT, MUSHY PULP

STARCH

10

Next, the paper is passed between two rotating cylinders that are just a fraction of a centimetre apart. This ensures that the paper is rolled to an even thinness all the way along.

11

The paper sheet passes under sprayers that pump out starch, which makes the paper whiter and stiffer. Another finishing called sizing is sprayed on: it helps the ink sit better on the paper when it is printed.

12

This single, continuous paper sheet is wound on to a giant steel spool. A machine cuts the reel into smaller ones.

13

The reels are rolled onto a sheeter, which unwinds the roll and cuts it into sheets of all sizes. The sheets are wrapped in plastic and piled on pallets, ready to be kept in a warehouse until they are ordered by shops and businesses.

Each reel of paper is around 80 kilometres long and 8.5 metres wide. The paper-making machine makes one of these giant reels every hour!

Turn the page to see how a book is made!

From Idea to Bookshelf

The journey of a book

What's your favourite book? Has it ever struck you that you are reading the very words the author wrote down, maybe late at night, sitting in their study? It's almost as though the story jumps straight from their head to yours. But what journey does the tale take in between?

1 Firstly, the author has a great idea for a story. She writes it all down. Then she reads it back and rewrites it, cutting parts she doesn't like and adding new sections. This stage can take up to a year or longer.

At last – a GREAT book. I want to represent this writer!

2 The story has been written. Now the author wants people to read it! Some authors publish books themselves but it costs a lot of money, so most try to find a publisher. First, they send their story to an agent. The agent understands the publishing industry, finds good authors for publishers, and makes sure that authors get paid properly.

4 At the publishing house, an editor reads the book. The editor knows a good story and can tell if other people will want to read it. He loves the book too!

5 He presents it to the publisher and the sales manager, who know which books are selling well at the moment. The publisher listens and makes the final decision. She agrees that this book should be published, so she writes to the agent offering the author a deal.

3 The agent sends the book to the right people at different publishing houses. This is a children's picture book, so she sends it to junior-fiction editors.

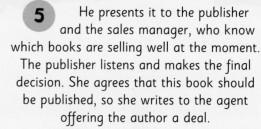

PUBLISHING HOUSE

6 Once the author, agent and publisher agree on a deal, they sign a contract that gives the publishing house the right to publish and sell the book.

The author is given a payment for the book, called an advance, and a percentage of every book sold, called a royalty.

7 An editor works on the book. The editor works with the author to make the story as good as possible. This may include cutting parts or adding new bits.

14 Bookshops will have already ordered copies of the book from the distribution centre. As soon as the copies arrive, they are sent out to the bookshops, where the staff unpack the books and put them on their shelves, ready for you to buy!

9 The cover designer works on making the cover look great. People really *do* judge a book by its cover, so a lot of time is spent getting it right. Then, the editor writes the back cover text. The cover has to be seen by everyone – especially the sales team, who know what customers want.

8 An illustrator draws the pictures. Then, a designer puts the pictures and text in the right places on the pages. The author and illustrator often don't meet, even when they are working on a book full of illustrations.

13 If the printer is in a different country, the finished books will be sent on a ship across the ocean. This can take a number of weeks. Finally, the books arrive at a port. They are unloaded and taken in a truck to a big book warehouse called a distribution centre.

10 The last person to check the text is the proofreader. He looks at every single detail of the book to make sure it is right: spellings, page numbers, paragraph indentations – everything!

11 The production controller sends the computer files to the printer with instructions about how the book should be printed. The printer makes proof, or test, copies for the publisher to make sure that everything is correct. Then, the production controller gives the printer the go-ahead to print all of the books.

12 The pages of the book are printed on giant rolls of paper, which are cut by special machines. The books are bound together with glue and thread.

At the click of a Button
The journey of your online shopping order

When you buy something in a shop, you take it to the till, pay for it and take your purchase home. But how does it work when you buy online? Let's look at what happens when you buy a birthday present for a friend.

4

Now the OMS communicates again through the server to your web browser to let you know that you have successfully purchased your item. You can go back to watching TV.

SHOP'S SERVER

BANK'S SERVER

3

If your item is available, the OMS communicates with the server of your dad's bank, asking for the money. The bank responds, telling it that money is available.

The OMS will use your postcode to look for your item in a warehouse as close to your home as possible.

1

You've found the perfect present online – a basketball. You click the 'Buy' button and add your delivery address. Your dad enters his credit card details to make the payment.

2

Your web browser communicates with a server (a very powerful computer) that manages the shop's website and Order Management System, or OMS – the shop's main computer system. The OMS checks to see whether the present you want to buy is available. Your item is somewhere far away in a large warehouse. If it is not available, an order for more is automatically sent to the supplier.

EXIT

13

In a day or so, your doorbell rings. A delivery driver is standing on your doorstep with your present, ready to wrap and take along to your friend's birthday party!

12

The parcels are packed onto lorries and taken to a shipment company. An email is sent to let you know your order has been dispatched.

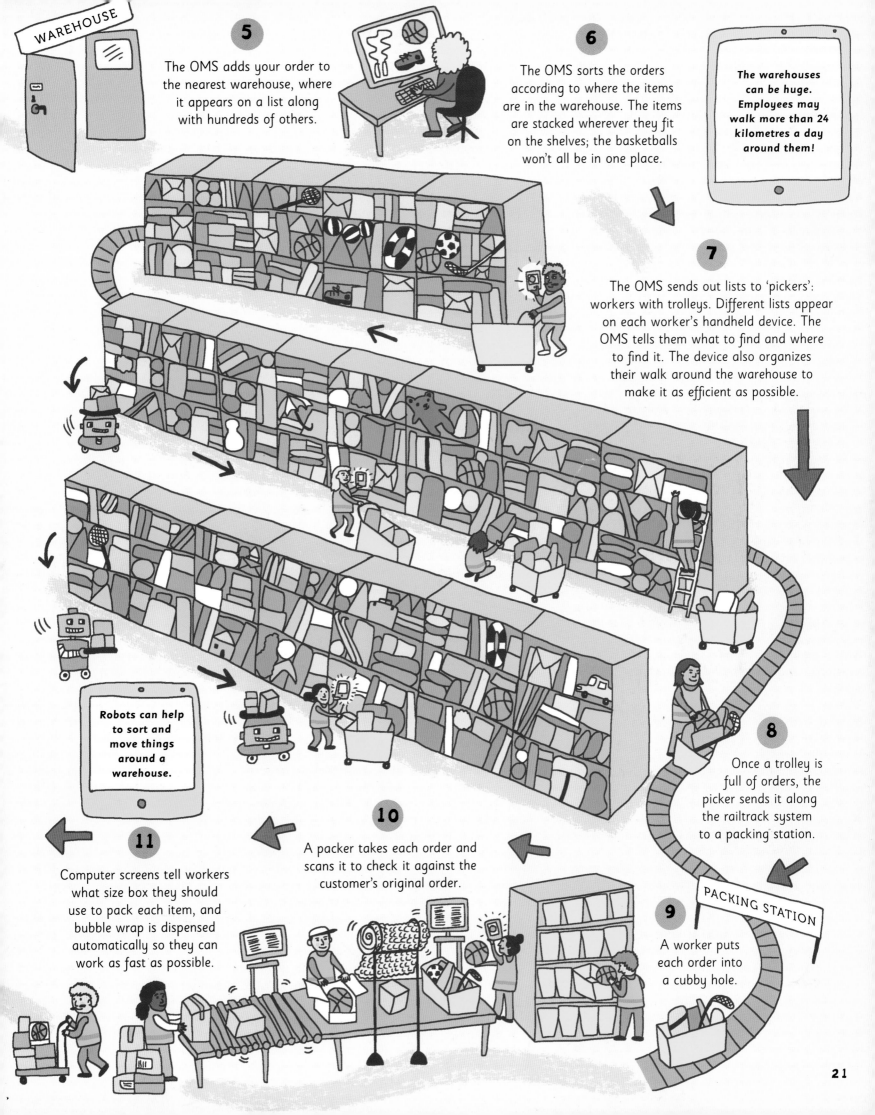

WAREHOUSE

5 The OMS adds your order to the nearest warehouse, where it appears on a list along with hundreds of others.

6 The OMS sorts the orders according to where the items are in the warehouse. The items are stacked wherever they fit on the shelves; the basketballs won't all be in one place.

The warehouses can be huge. Employees may walk more than 24 kilometres a day around them!

7 The OMS sends out lists to 'pickers': workers with trolleys. Different lists appear on each worker's handheld device. The OMS tells them what to find and where to find it. The device also organizes their walk around the warehouse to make it as efficient as possible.

Robots can help to sort and move things around a warehouse.

8 Once a trolley is full of orders, the picker sends it along the railtrack system to a packing station.

11 Computer screens tell workers what size box they should use to pack each item, and bubble wrap is dispensed automatically so they can work as fast as possible.

10 A packer takes each order and scans it to check it against the customer's original order.

PACKING STATION

9 A worker puts each order into a cubby hole.

How Glass Never Dies

The journey of a used glass bottle

A glass bottle you recycle can be made into new bottles forever. Turning it back into new glass saves resources, energy and money. Here's what happens.

1

The bin collectors pick up your recycling and take it to a Materials Recycling Facility (MRF), where the glass, metal, paper and plastics are separated.

The energy saved from recycling just one bottle can power a computer for 25 minutes!

13

After they cool, the bottles are sold to a lemonade factory, where they are filled, lidded and sent to the shop for you to buy, use and recycle all over again.

12 The liquid glass is divided into soft cylinder shapes, called gobs, which are dropped into moulds. Air is blown into the middle of the gob, hollowing out the inside and forming the shape of the bottle.

11

At a glass bottle factory, the cullet is melted in a furnace at temperatures of around 1,500°C (about six times hotter than a hot oven at home). Materials, including sand, are added to turn the glass into liquid.

2 The glass is taken to the recycling plant for processing. It passes around the plant on a conveyor belt.

3 In some plants, the glass is washed to get rid of old food or mould.

4 The glass moves under powerful magnets, which pull out any large pieces of metal, such as tin cans or bottle lids, still mixed with the glass.

6 The conveyor belt reaches the drier. Hot air passes over the glass until not a drop of moisture remains. Any paper labels loosen and fall off.

5 Workers sort the glass by hand and pick out any other objects or very dirty pieces.

7 A huge vacuum sucks up any small objects that have managed to get through to this point: labels, bottle corks, dust and bits of plastic or paper.

8 Further along, laser cameras scan the colour of the glass. Jets of air blast the main three different colours into separate containers.

In the UK, around half of all glass is recycled.

Rinse your glass bottles before you put them in the recycling so that the waste inside doesn't mould and smell bad.

9 The factory names for the three main glass colours are amber (brown), green (green!) and flint (clear).

Not all glass can be recycled. Some kinds, such as oven dishes and window glass, are made differently to bottles. The conveyor belt passes under laser cameras that scan the glass. The cameras detect any pieces that cannot be recycled and wash them away with a jet of high-pressured air.

10 The glass is crushed into little pieces called cullet. Glass manufacturers buy cullet to turn it back into new glass.

Cullet melts at a lower temperature than new glass made from raw materials, using 40% less energy.

From Tree to Tummy
The journey of chocolate

Did you know that chocolate comes from a fruit? Here's how it gets from a tree in a tropical rainforest to a wrapper on a shelf in your local shop.

The scientific name for the cacao tree is Theobroma cacao, which means 'food of the gods'.

1

Chocolate begins in a cacao pod, the fruit of the cacao tree. The trees grow mostly in hot, tropical areas close to the Equator.

Each cacao tree produces around 30 pods a year. The fruit grows from the trunk and branches.

2

When the fruit is ripe, it is cut from the tree by hand using a long-handled hook. The cacao pod has a thick, leathery rind that can be red, yellow or green. Inside is a sweet, gluey pulp surrounding the soft cacao seeds. It tastes a bit like lemonade!

3

The seeds are taken out, heaped into a pile and covered in banana leaves to warm up and ferment. This takes around six days.

While fermenting, the pulp around the cacao seeds becomes liquid and drains away, and the chocolate flavour begins to develop.

4

Then, the beans are laid out in the sunshine to dry for another few days.

5

Now the farmers can sell their beans at a cacao-bean market. The beans are weighed, tested for quality, and then sold on to chocolate-processing plants all over the world.

6

At the chocolate-processing plant, machines take over. Here's a simplified version. The beans are tipped onto a conveyor belt, which carries them along...

...while they are washed...

...roasted under a hot air blast...

...kibbled (broken up into small pieces)...

...and winnowed (the hard bits of shell are blown away, leaving the soft inside of the bean, known as the nib).

7 The nibs are ground up until they make a soft, creamy paste known as chocolate mass. This is the basic ingredient used in all chocolate products, but it doesn't taste sweet yet.

Chocolate mass can be pressed and strained, separating the natural fat from the solid. The fat is cocoa butter. The solid is cocoa powder, which is used in drinking chocolate or for baking.

9 The blocks are ground up and mixed into a paste with other ingredients. Different amounts of milk, sugar and vanilla are added to the mass to make white, milk or dark chocolate. Dark chocolate has lots of cocoa powder in it. White chocolate has no cocoa powder, only cocoa butter.

SUGAR

MILK

VANILLA

8 Next, the chocolate mass is delivered to chocolate factories in blocks, ready to be made into yummy, sweet chocolate.

CHOCOLATE FACTORY

10 The paste is melted and churned to turn it into a smooth liquid.

11 Next, the paste is cooled down in vats so that little fat and sugar crystals develop. This makes the chocolate smooth.

12 When it is ready, the runny chocolate is dropped into moulds, shaken to remove air bubbles, and chilled until hard.

13 Finally, the chocolate is wrapped, packed into boxes...

14 ...collected by lorries, and delivered to your local shop, ready for you to buy with your pocket money!

25

Where Does My Luggage Go when I catch a Plane?
The journey of a suitcase

You've got your tickets, packed your bags and you're at the airport, ready for your holiday – how exciting! Your suitcase will be taking a little trip of its own...

1

When you arrive at the airport, you will have baggage – a large bag containing items to take on vacation. The baggage needs to go in the hold of the plane – a big space in the belly of the plane. You may also have hand-luggage with a few things you'll need during the flight.

Many airports now have self-service check-in points too.

2

The check-in agent registers that you have arrived for your flight. They also weigh your bag. You will already have been told how heavy your bag is allowed to be when you bought the plane tickets. If all the passengers turned up with very heavy bags, the plane wouldn't be able to get off the ground!

8.25 KG

3

The agent attaches a tag with a barcode to your bag. This has all the information about your flight on it, so the baggage handlers know which plane to put it on.

8

Next, each bag travels through a large X-ray machine to be screened and checked for dangerous objects.

9

Airports are enormous places, and sometimes baggage has to go a long way to get from the check-in area to its plane. If so, it might be tipped into a little trolley and whisked along at high speed on tracks that go up and down like a mini-rollercoaster. Wheee!

At this point, 'transfer luggage' is added. These bags belong to passengers changing planes to join your flight.

10

The trolley tips your bag from a high conveyor belt down a slope, a bit like a curly slide, to the 'reconciliation' area at the bottom. There, an employee scans the barcode to match your bag to your flight, and loads it onto a large container.

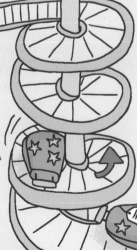

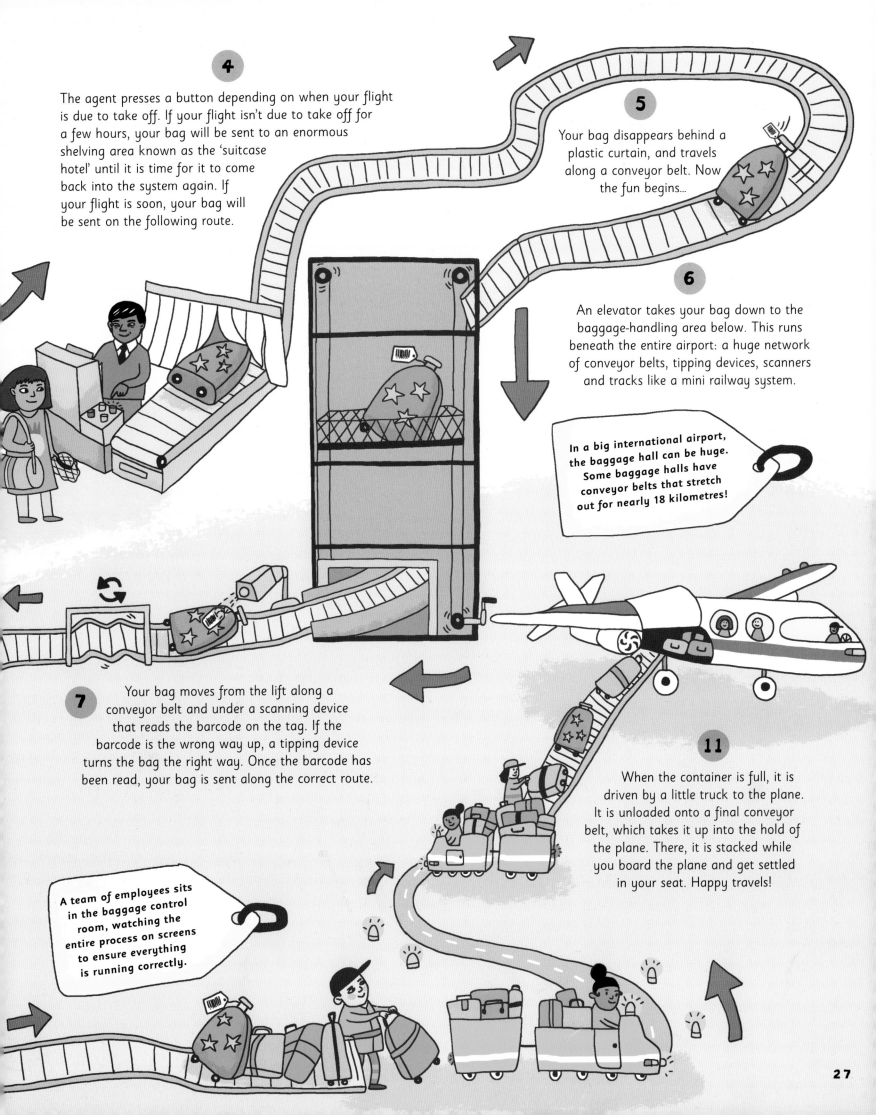

4

The agent presses a button depending on when your flight is due to take off. If your flight isn't due to take off for a few hours, your bag will be sent to an enormous shelving area known as the 'suitcase hotel' until it is time for it to come back into the system again. If your flight is soon, your bag will be sent on the following route.

5

Your bag disappears behind a plastic curtain, and travels along a conveyor belt. Now the fun begins...

6

An elevator takes your bag down to the baggage-handling area below. This runs beneath the entire airport: a huge network of conveyor belts, tipping devices, scanners and tracks like a mini railway system.

In a big international airport, the baggage hall can be huge. Some baggage halls have conveyor belts that stretch out for nearly 18 kilometres!

7

Your bag moves from the lift along a conveyor belt and under a scanning device that reads the barcode on the tag. If the barcode is the wrong way up, a tipping device turns the bag the right way. Once the barcode has been read, your bag is sent along the correct route.

A team of employees sits in the baggage control room, watching the entire process on screens to ensure everything is running correctly.

11

When the container is full, it is driven by a little truck to the plane. It is unloaded onto a final conveyor belt, which takes it up into the hold of the plane. There, it is stacked while you board the plane and get settled in your seat. Happy travels!

where Does the water in the Tap come from?

A journey through the water cycle

2

The vapour rose... higher and higher... until it reached cold air. The cold air turned the vapour back into water droplets. They hung there, high in the sky, forming a cloud. When water vapour cools and becomes liquid again, it is called condensation.

As it evaporates, the water leaves behind anything mixed with it, such as salt or dirt. The water becomes pure.

3

As more and more droplets gathered, the bigger and darker the cloud became. It grew so heavy with water that the droplets fell to the ground again as rain. (When it's very cold, water falls as snow.) Falling rain or snow is called precipitation.

Before you start reading, get a glass of water. The water has travelled the world and been around for billions of years. Just last year, it was probably in one of the oceans, rivers and lakes that make up about three-quarters of Earth's surface.

1

Last summer, the sun shone on the ocean. It warmed the water droplets on the surface until they turned from a liquid into a gas, called water vapour. This process is called evaporation. The vapour rose into the air.

Rain also falls into lakes and reservoirs – artificial lakes created for storing water. In cities, it flows from street gutters down into storm drains, and then into rivers.

CUTAWAY OF GROUND

4

The falling rain trickled down in streams until it found its way into the ground. The water flowed down through the ground into the spaces between the rocks, until it joined big underground pools called aquifers.

AQUI

28

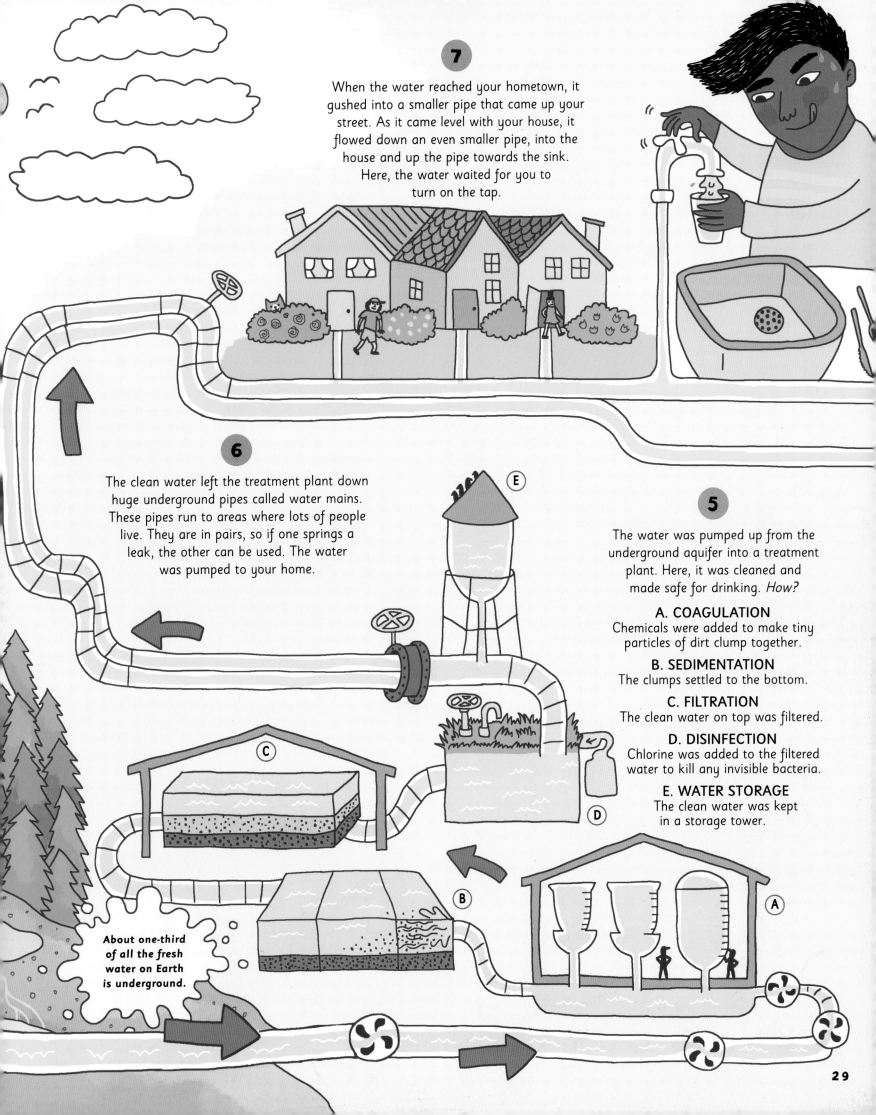

7

When the water reached your hometown, it gushed into a smaller pipe that came up your street. As it came level with your house, it flowed down an even smaller pipe, into the house and up the pipe towards the sink. Here, the water waited for you to turn on the tap.

6

The clean water left the treatment plant down huge underground pipes called water mains. These pipes run to areas where lots of people live. They are in pairs, so if one springs a leak, the other can be used. The water was pumped to your home.

5

The water was pumped up from the underground aquifer into a treatment plant. Here, it was cleaned and made safe for drinking. *How?*

A. COAGULATION
Chemicals were added to make tiny particles of dirt clump together.

B. SEDIMENTATION
The clumps settled to the bottom.

C. FILTRATION
The clean water on top was filtered.

D. DISINFECTION
Chlorine was added to the filtered water to kill any invisible bacteria.

E. WATER STORAGE
The clean water was kept in a storage tower.

About one-third of all the fresh water on Earth is underground.

From Fossil to car
The journey of petrol

Have you ever heard of fossil fuels? A fuel is a material that is burned to produce heat and power. A fossil is the remains of a prehistoric plant or animal that has become embedded in layers of rock. We use a substance that is millions and millions of years old to run some of our most modern technology.

1

Between 550 and 65 million years ago, plants and animals died and sank to the bottom of the ocean. Over time, they were covered by mud.

2

The mud preserved them for many thousands of years. In that time, oceans dried up, volcanoes erupted, and the mud became a layer of rock. The preserved organic (plant and animal) matter was trapped. It decomposed, slowly, until millions of years later it had become a sticky black liquid called crude oil. The oil produced a gas called natural gas. Both the oil and gas smell a bit like rotten eggs.

Crude oil and natural gas provide most of our fuel. But they can be as far as 13 kilometres underground!

3

Crude oil is worth a lot of money. It is found around the world, and oil companies spend a lot of time and effort looking for it. Geologists use 'seismic' technology: shock waves sent into the ground that bounce off the layers of rock and back to the surface, indicating what lies below.

4

Once companies have found oil, they build large platforms called oil rigs. These may be on land or at sea. If there is a huge supply, oil could be pumped there for many years. An enormous drill is used to penetrate deep into the ground.

5

The drill uses a diamond tip, one of the hardest substances on Earth, to penetrate through the rock layers. As it whizzes round, the friction creates a vast amount of heat. This would be dangerous if it hit explosive gas, so a kind of muddy water is continually pumped down through the rock to cool everything down.

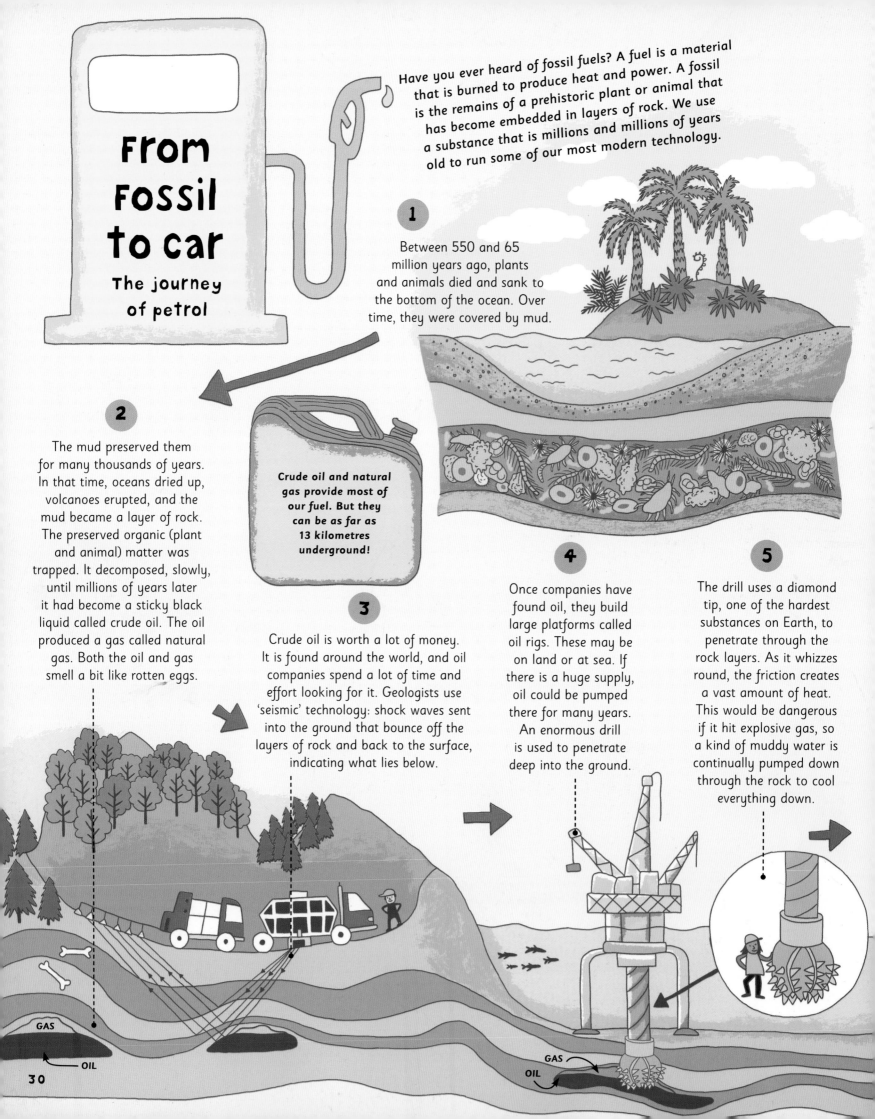

GAS

OIL

GAS

OIL

When petrol is burned, it releases lots of carbon dioxide, one of the main gases that is causing Earth's temperature to rise.

10 The petrol is collected from the terminal by tankers, and driven to petrol stations in that area. The workers pour the petrol through a hose into a large tank beneath the pumps.

11 Before very long, it is pumped up through one of the hoses under the pump and into the petrol tank of a car – maybe your family's car?

A. GAS
B. PETROL
C. KEROSENE
D. DIESEL OIL
E. FUEL OIL
F. LUBRICATING OIL, PARAFFIN WAX AND ASPHALT
G. CRUDE OIL
H. FURNACE

9 The petrol is transported through a series of underground pipes to terminals all around the country. These are large storage tanks close to towns and cities.

Oil is also used to make car tyres, life jackets, tents, cameras, footballs, paint, bin bags, crayons, contact lenses and even beauty products.

Every year, billions of barrels of crude oil are pumped up from beneath the ground.

6 Machines called 'nodding donkeys' act like giant syringes, pumping oil up to the surface.

Oil is transported across the sea in huge ships called tankers.

OIL REFINERY

7 From the surface, the oil is sent hundreds of kilometres down long pipes to oil refineries for processing.

8 At the oil refinery, the oil is heated in a giant furnace. As it warms, different elements of it rise to the surface and are sucked out at the level to which they've risen. Near the top is petrol.

GAS

OIL

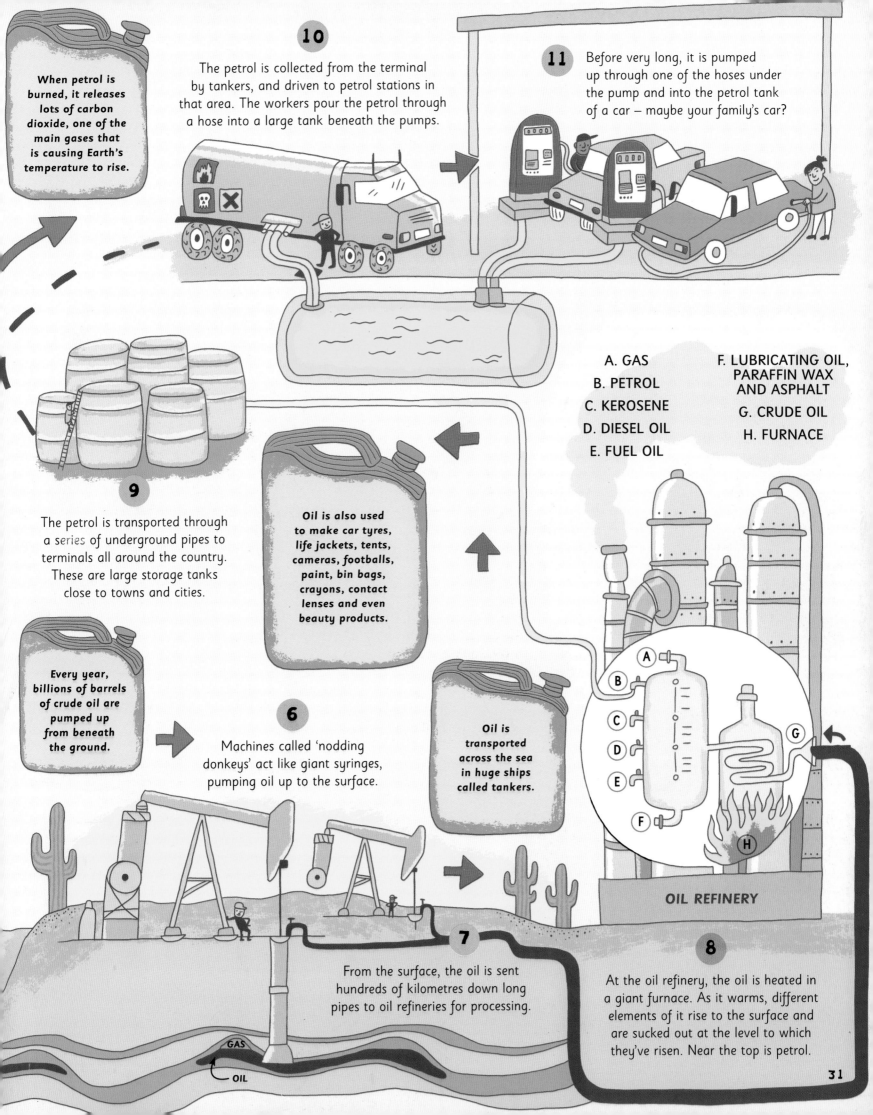

The Invisible Movement of Millions

The journey of money

Would you believe that money in today's online world is just an idea that we all believe in? Let's see how we got here.

1

Money is a currency, which is something you can use to trade with. Thousands of years ago, we traded with commodities – useful things. People might have traded a bag of salt for some beans or a cow for a tool. This is called commodity currency.

2

But cows died and beans could go mouldy. Over time, swapping things was replaced by swapping gold. Gold was a metal available all over the world, it didn't go bad and was soft enough to form into coins. Silver soon joined it. This was known as coin currency.

3

But metal was heavy to carry around, so people left it with gold traders, who gave them a receipt for it. If your receipt was for five silver coins, you could trade it for something worth that much. This was called paper currency.

4

Gold and silver traders grew to become banks that looked after people's money for them. The customer could withdraw it when they needed, or deposit more. These transactions (movements of money) were written in account books so everyone could keep track.

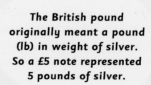

The British pound originally meant a pound (lb) in weight of silver. So a £5 note represented 5 pounds of silver.

5

These days, account books have been replaced by sophisticated computer systems. You don't need to see the gold or silver those numbers represent any longer; you don't even need to see the paper money. The currency no longer needs to be visible or even exist as a physical object. You can transfer money electronically. Let's look at an example of how money is transferred electronically.

Shops, employers, skilled workers and even governments use electronic bank transfers to trade billions of pounds every day. It's estimated that only 8 per cent of the world's currency exists as physical cash.

6 MONDAY

Your mum goes to work every day. At the end of the month, her employer's bank tells your mum's bank that it has paid her. The balance (amount of money) goes up in your mum's bank account and down in her employer's account, but no notes or coins have been exchanged. This is an electronic bank transfer.

ITEM	DEBIT	CREDIT	BALANCE
Work		£800	£800
Electricity	£50		£800
ATM Withdrawal	£20		£750
Supermarket	£30		£730
Shoe Shop	£25		£700
			£675

7 TUESDAY

Your mum needs to pay some bills – say, the electricity. The electricity company informs the bank how much your mum should pay and the bank does another electronic bank transfer. The balance goes down in her bank account and up in the account of the electricity company.

10 FRIDAY

Your mum goes online to buy you a new pair of school shoes. She enters the details of her card on the website page, which tells her bank that she wants to transfer some of her money to the online shop. Since being paid, your mum has spent more than £100, and most of the money has been exchanged electronically.

8 WEDNESDAY

Now your mum needs to pay £20 for your sports club. The club asks for cash. She goes to an Automatic Teller Machine (ATM) with her card. When she puts in the card, the ATM reads the magnetic strip. Once she enters the correct Personal Identification Number (PIN) code, she accesses the computer system of her bank. The money taken out at the ATM is recorded by her bank.

9 THURSDAY

You and your mum go shopping, and she uses her card. She spends £30. The shop's computer system communicates with the bank's computer system, and the money is transferred from her bank account to the shop's account.

The journey of a film from script to screen

Behind almost every film you see are months – even years – of hard work by a team of people. Follow the journey of a film idea.

1 This writer has had a great idea for a film. But he can't make it all by himself. He needs to pay for actors, costumes, set design, camera and lighting equipment, travel...

2 The writer has a meeting with a producer, and explains all about his idea for the film. This is called a 'pitch'.

7 The film is advertised and the stars give interviews to promote it. There may be a premiere – a first showing of the film with a party. The writer's idea has travelled from his imagination to the imagination of other people, and has become a reality!

A film may be released in different parts of the world at different times, in cinemas or straight to DVD or on-demand providers.

6 Now all the footage has to be put together in the right order, using the best bits, taking out the parts that didn't work so well, and adding special effects, music, credits and any voice-over recordings. The film editor and the director do this work on computers.

Cast List

WRITER

PRODUCER

DIRECTOR

DIRECTOR OF PHOTOGRAPHY (DP)

ACTOR 1

ACTOR 2

3 If the producer likes the idea, they agree to make a sample of the film. This is called a 'treatment'. Films cost a lot of money to make so the producer needs to persuade people to invest money in it.

4 The producer has found the money and has a screenplay (the script with instructions for the actors), but now needs to hire a director and actors.

5 Finally it's time to shoot the film! The producer hires a huge crew of people. They all have a different job to do on set. This includes camera operators, make-up artists, costume-makers and sound and lighting engineers. Shooting the film might take a whole year!

The scenes of the film are not filmed in the order in which they appear. If there are several scenes set in the same place, these will be filmed at the same time, even if they are from different parts of the story.

How Does the Internet Work?

The superfast journey of information

The Internet is the network that links all of the computers in the world to each other. It's made up of all kinds of computers, tablets and smartphones. Say you want to find a picture on the Internet of your favourite dog, the labradoodle. How does the photo reach you?

1

In a search engine, such as Google, you type in 'labradoodle' and click on 'images'. You see a cute picture that you want to download and click on it.

3 Your request for the labradoodle picture is sent to your Internet Service Provider (ISP), the company you pay for your Internet service. The ISP has lots of servers to store and transfer data. Servers are very powerful computers, which contain far more information than our home computers. They can be anywhere in the world.

The Internet is the network of all the computers in the world. The World Wide Web is all the information on those computers that travels around the Internet.

2

Your computer, phone or tablet is linked to the Internet through a modem, a jumping-off point to the worldwide network of computers.

Every computer and server has an address of ten numbers called an Internet Protocol (IP) address.

4

Your ISP sends a request to the IP address of the server that has the image. It might be in another country. It finds the speediest way to reach the server with that IP address. Your request might travel along fibre-optic cables under the ocean or via a satellite in space. Along the way, your request goes through more computers called routers, switches or hubs, which are like stations on the Internet.

You can look up an IP address on a Domain Name Server, which is like a giant address book.

5

All information on the Internet is broken down and sent in small 'packets' so it can travel faster. Along the way, the packets are separated. Every time a packet reaches a new hub, switch or router, it is sent on the fastest route available.

6

When the packets reach the IP address that asked for the information, the computer puts them back together again in the correct order.

7

Your request reaches the server that has the image you want. The server sends the image to your computer. This all happens in less than a second!

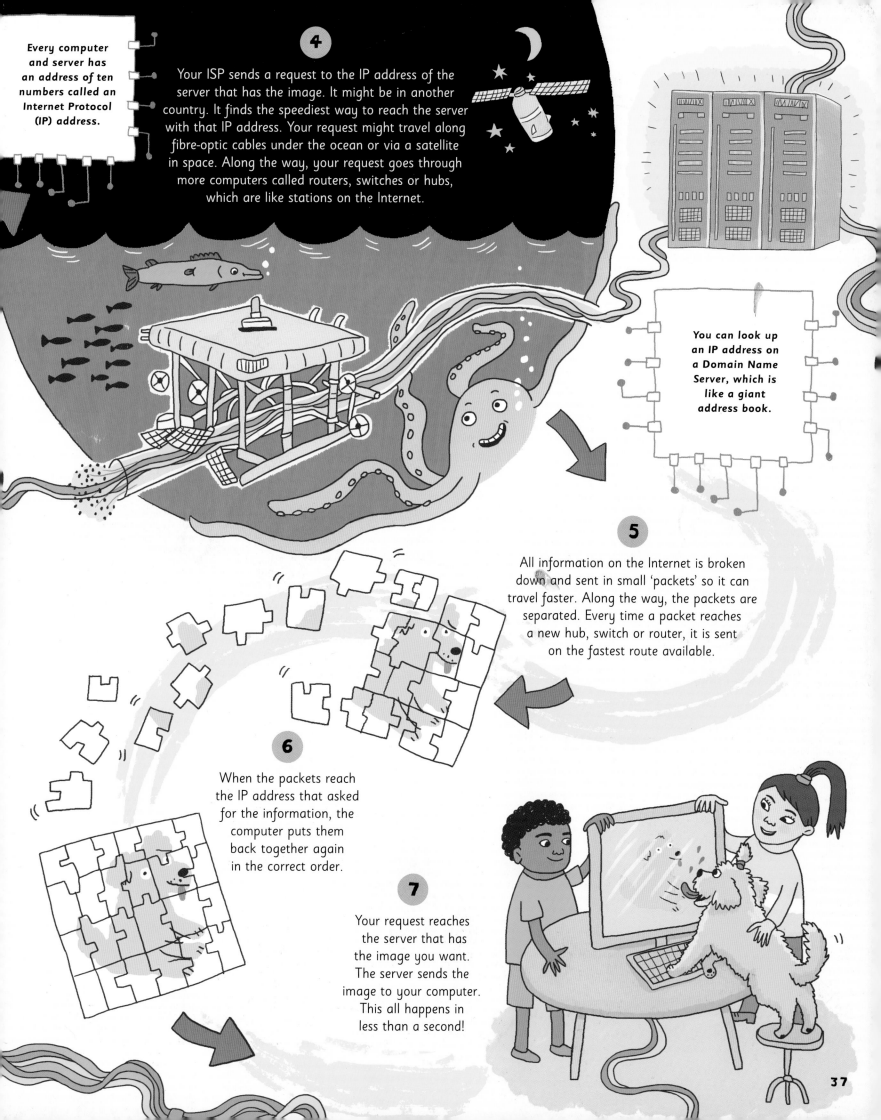

From studio to stereo

The journey of music

What's your favourite song? How do you listen to it? Does the singer perform it in your room? (It's unlikely although not impossible.) So how can you hear it as though the singer was in the room with you? How was that song captured?

Sound waves travel a certain distance before running out of energy. If the sound waves reach you, the sounds are 'within earshot'. If they cannot reach you, you're 'out of earshot'.

RAREFACTION

COMPRESSION

WAVELENGTH

1

As a singer's vocal cords open and close, they move back and forth, vibrating very quickly. When they close, they compress (squash) the molecules in the air together. When they open, they let the air 'rarefact' (spread out again). These squashing and expanding movements pass on from air molecule to air molecule, rippling out. This is called a sound wave.

2

A microphone has a cone-shaped piece of plastic called a diaphragm in it that works a bit like vocal cords in reverse. The diaphragm vibrates with the rise and fall of the sound waves and converts those vibrations into electrical signals that rise and fall in the same pattern. The electrical signals can be recorded in different ways – **analogue** or **digital**.

RECORDING

The best way to capture as many sound waves as possible is to get right in front of their source. Your singer was probably in a booth in a recording studio, a tiny room that traps the waves, with a microphone right in front of their mouth. The booth traps the waves and deflects them back again so that the microphone can capture as many as possible and get the full impact of the singer's voice.

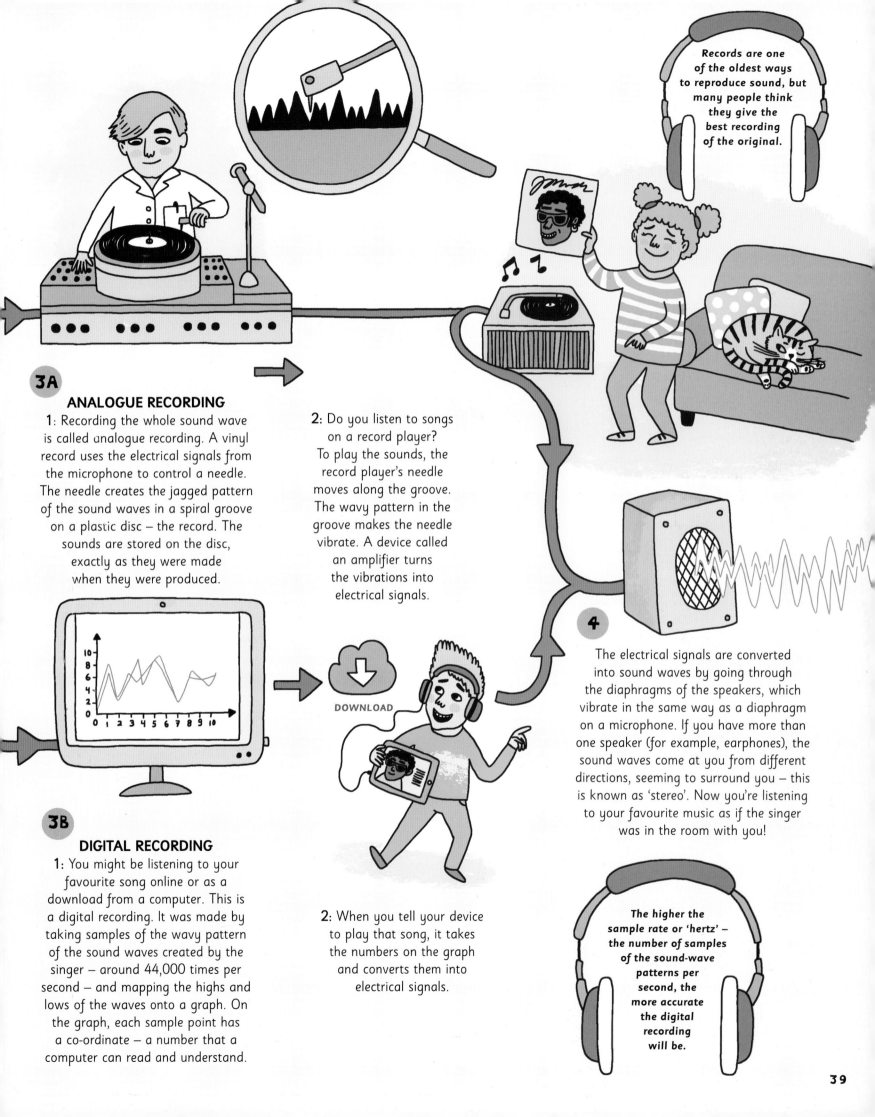

3A

ANALOGUE RECORDING

1: Recording the whole sound wave is called analogue recording. A vinyl record uses the electrical signals from the microphone to control a needle. The needle creates the jagged pattern of the sound waves in a spiral groove on a plastic disc – the record. The sounds are stored on the disc, exactly as they were made when they were produced.

2: Do you listen to songs on a record player? To play the sounds, the record player's needle moves along the groove. The wavy pattern in the groove makes the needle vibrate. A device called an amplifier turns the vibrations into electrical signals.

3B

DIGITAL RECORDING

1: You might be listening to your favourite song online or as a download from a computer. This is a digital recording. It was made by taking samples of the wavy pattern of the sound waves created by the singer – around 44,000 times per second – and mapping the highs and lows of the waves onto a graph. On the graph, each sample point has a co-ordinate – a number that a computer can read and understand.

DOWNLOAD

2: When you tell your device to play that song, it takes the numbers on the graph and converts them into electrical signals.

4

The electrical signals are converted into sound waves by going through the diaphragms of the speakers, which vibrate in the same way as a diaphragm on a microphone. If you have more than one speaker (for example, earphones), the sound waves come at you from different directions, seeming to surround you – this is known as 'stereo'. Now you're listening to your favourite music as if the singer was in the room with you!

The higher the sample rate or 'hertz' – the number of samples of the sound-wave patterns per second, the more accurate the digital recording will be.

39

WHERE DO the words GO?

The journey of a phone call

A woman in the city is talking on her mobile phone to a friend who is walking through a field on the other side of the country. How do her words reach that far? Let's follow them.

1 When the woman speaks, the words come out as a series of vibrations, which travel out of her mouth as sound waves (see page 38 for more information). Off they go in all directions. Many will go into the ears of people nearby.

2 But she's talking to someone too far away for the sound waves to reach. Inside the phone, a tiny microphone picks up the sound waves and copies the pattern they make into a matching electrical signal.

3 A microchip (like a tiny computer) converts the electrical signal into a digital code — a set of numbers.

Analogue is when a sound wave – such as your voice – is recorded in its original form. Digital is when an analogue sound is recorded and then turned into a set of numbers.

4 The antenna inside the phone transmits (sends) this digital code on radio waves. These radio waves race through the air at the speed of light (300,000 kilometres per second).

5 The radio waves reach the nearest phone mast. There are lots of masts in cities, but fewer in the countryside because there are not as many people. The phone mast picks up the radio waves and passes it along to the base station.

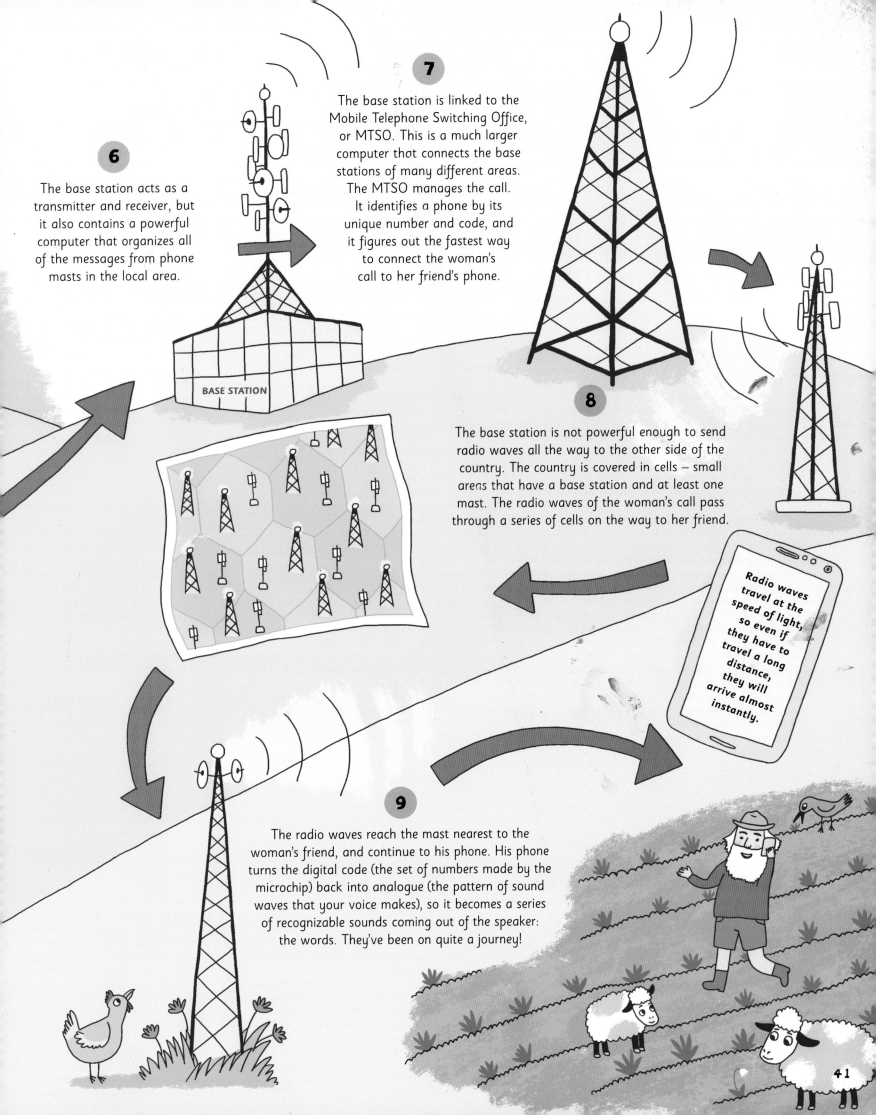

6

The base station acts as a transmitter and receiver, but it also contains a powerful computer that organizes all of the messages from phone masts in the local area.

7

The base station is linked to the Mobile Telephone Switching Office, or MTSO. This is a much larger computer that connects the base stations of many different areas. The MTSO manages the call. It identifies a phone by its unique number and code, and it figures out the fastest way to connect the woman's call to her friend's phone.

BASE STATION

8

The base station is not powerful enough to send radio waves all the way to the other side of the country. The country is covered in cells — small areas that have a base station and at least one mast. The radio waves of the woman's call pass through a series of cells on the way to her friend.

Radio waves travel at the speed of light, so even if they have to travel a long distance, they will arrive almost instantly.

9

The radio waves reach the mast nearest to the woman's friend, and continue to his phone. His phone turns the digital code (the set of numbers made by the microchip) back into analogue (the pattern of sound waves that your voice makes), so it becomes a series of recognizable sounds coming out of the speaker: the words. They've been on quite a journey!

41

We use electricity with barely a thought – flick a switch and it's there! But where does it come from? Electricity is a form of energy. In the early 19th century, British scientist Michael Faraday discovered he could create electricity. If he moved a magnet around a loop of wire, the wire became electrified. This is called 'electromagnetic induction'. We still produce electricity in the same way.

What Makes the Lights Go On?

The journey of electricity

A-ha!

Electricity is produced by power stations all around the world. Inside are many enormous generators ('generate' means to create). They work in the same way as Faraday's experiment, except now they have giant magnets turning around massive wire loops.

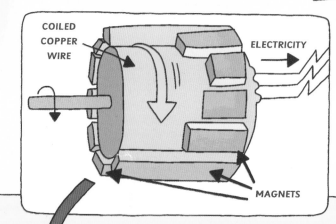

COILED COPPER WIRE

ELECTRICITY

MAGNETS

2

First, power is needed to move the turbines that turn the magnets. Turbines are machines which capture energy from moving water or steam. Different types of power stations use different primary sources of energy to create electricity.

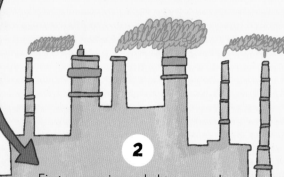

(A) FOSSIL-FUEL POWER STATIONS
burn coal, natural gas or oil from the ground to boil water. When water boils, it produces steam. The steam rotates the turbines of the generators. This is the cheapest form of fuel and produces most of the world's electricity.

(E) SOLAR-POWER STATIONS
convert energy from the sun's rays directly into electricity. But adapting the electricity grid to work with solar-power stations is expensive, so there aren't many of them.

(B) WIND AND HYDROELECTRIC POWER STATIONS
use the power of moving wind and water to turn the turbines of the generators.

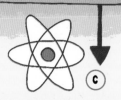

(C) NUCLEAR POWER STATIONS
split atoms. This creates heat to boil water and produce steam to turn the turbines of the generators.

(D) GEOTHERMAL POWER STATIONS
use heat from the centre of Earth to boil water that produces steam to turn the turbines. This is only possible in places where this heat is near the surface of Earth.

4

The electricity might travel long distances across the grid until it reaches a distribution centre.

The grid is a network of wires that allows the electricity to travel where it is needed. These wires travel above ground, held up by towers called pylons, or are buried under the ground. They travel between countries and even continents – electricity produced in the UK could power a home in the US.

3

The electricity leaves the power station and flows into a step-up transformer that increases its voltage (strength).

STEP-UP TRANSFORMER

DISTRIBUTION CENTRE

5

From the distribution centre, the voltage is distributed around the area that the energy company supplies. The wires it travels along are called distribution lines.

Electricity flows a bit like water around circuits – in closed loops. When a switch is off, the loop has a tiny gap in it and the electricity cannot flow through. When a switch is turned on, the loop is closed and the electricity can flow.

6

Electricity at a lower voltage is carried on power lines to businesses and homes.

7

Next time you go to turn on electricity in your house, pause a moment. Remember that when you push that switch, you complete the circuit. The electricity zipping along the wires past your house suddenly has another circuit to travel along, and will flow around it. Think about where that electricity might have begun, and how you are about to send it on the final part of its journey...

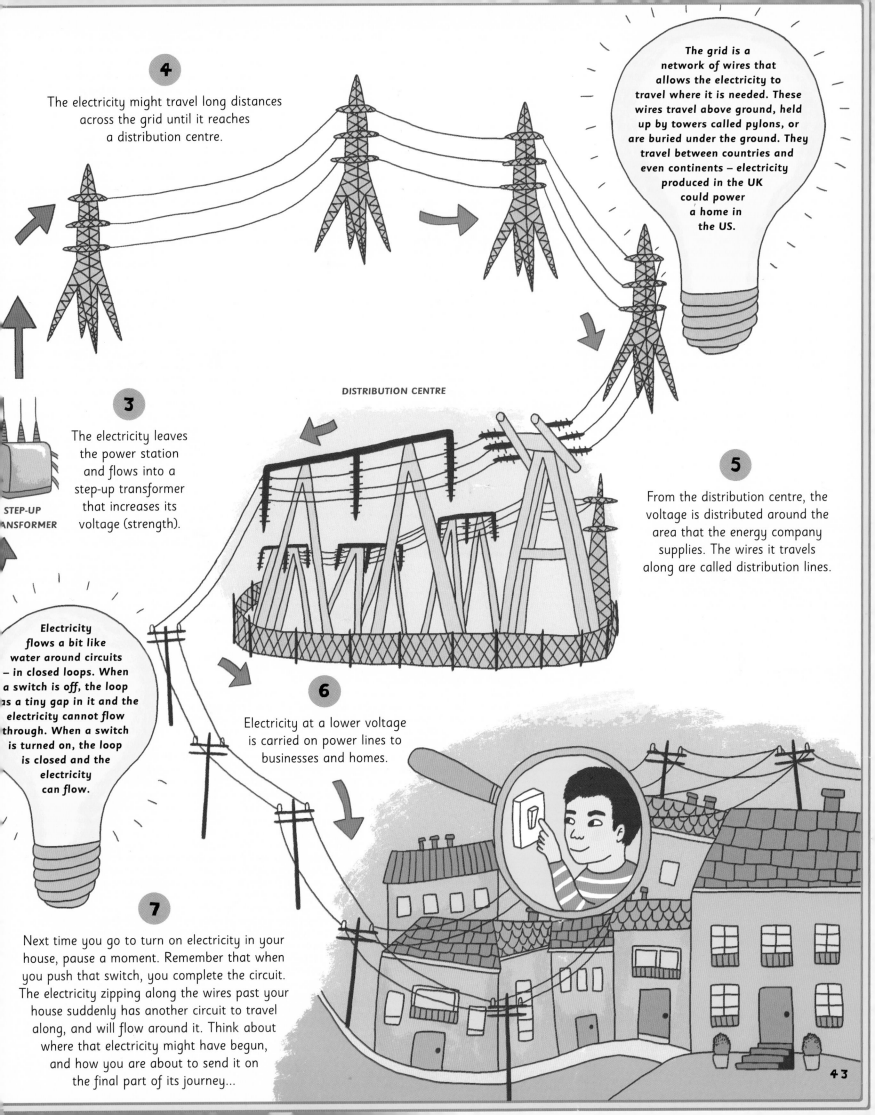

43

What Happens When I Flush?
The journey of poo

Ah, those familiar sounds: plop... splash... flush! Everybody knows them well... but how many people know what happens to their poo once it's disappeared around the U-bend? Read on...

1

So you've just flushed and now you're washing your hands (hopefully). Meanwhile, your poo is zipping at high speed down a pipe on the side of the building and along another pipe to the street.

The U-bend means some water is always trapped in the bend under your toilet after the smelly stuff has been flushed away. This stops stinky smells coming back up through the pipe – the water acts like a plug.

Sewage treatment plants are usually on the outskirts of towns and cities, partly because they take up a lot of space, but also because of the funky smell!

TREATMENT PLANT

2

The sewage pipe from your house joins a bigger sewage pipe that travels under the road. Your little poo bobs along into that and is swept along with all the dirty dishwater, bathwater, poos and pees from your neighbours' houses.

PUMPING STATION

3

This pipe joins an even bigger pipe. The sewage (waste) flows using gravity along a large network of pipes out to a sewage treatment plant. If it has to go uphill, it sometimes needs to go through a pumping station to keep it moving along.

11

The remaining water is now clean enough to be sent to a river or the ocean. There, it becomes part of the water cycle. Eventually, it will form clouds and fall as rain. And we know what happens to it next! (See pages 28 and 29 for a reminder.)

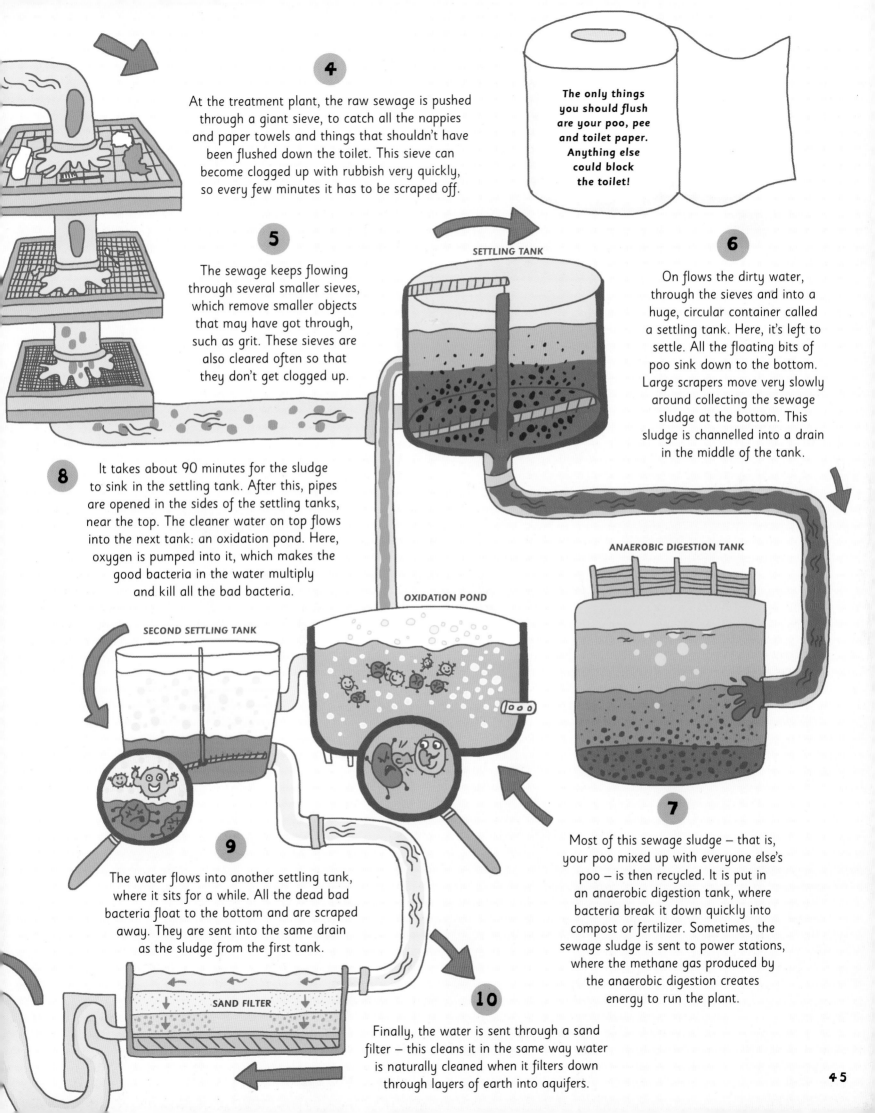

4

At the treatment plant, the raw sewage is pushed through a giant sieve, to catch all the nappies and paper towels and things that shouldn't have been flushed down the toilet. This sieve can become clogged up with rubbish very quickly, so every few minutes it has to be scraped off.

The only things you should flush are your poo, pee and toilet paper. Anything else could block the toilet!

5

The sewage keeps flowing through several smaller sieves, which remove smaller objects that may have got through, such as grit. These sieves are also cleared often so that they don't get clogged up.

SETTLING TANK

6

On flows the dirty water, through the sieves and into a huge, circular container called a settling tank. Here, it's left to settle. All the floating bits of poo sink down to the bottom. Large scrapers move very slowly around collecting the sewage sludge at the bottom. This sludge is channelled into a drain in the middle of the tank.

8

It takes about 90 minutes for the sludge to sink in the settling tank. After this, pipes are opened in the sides of the settling tanks, near the top. The cleaner water on top flows into the next tank: an oxidation pond. Here, oxygen is pumped into it, which makes the good bacteria in the water multiply and kill all the bad bacteria.

ANAEROBIC DIGESTION TANK

OXIDATION POND

SECOND SETTLING TANK

9

The water flows into another settling tank, where it sits for a while. All the dead bad bacteria float to the bottom and are scraped away. They are sent into the same drain as the sludge from the first tank.

7

Most of this sewage sludge – that is, your poo mixed up with everyone else's poo – is then recycled. It is put in an anaerobic digestion tank, where bacteria break it down quickly into compost or fertilizer. Sometimes, the sewage sludge is sent to power stations, where the methane gas produced by the anaerobic digestion creates energy to run the plant.

SAND FILTER

10

Finally, the water is sent through a sand filter – this cleans it in the same way water is naturally cleaned when it filters down through layers of earth into aquifers.

from cow to carton

The journey of milk

We all know that milk comes from a cow and that it is used to make cheese, butter and other dairy foods. But when you pour that carton of milk over your cereal, do you ever think about the journey it has made to get there?

1

Milk is made in a cow's body from food and water. Dairy cows drink about a bathtub of water and eat about 50 kilograms of food every day — the weight of 1,500 servings of your breakfast cereal. They mostly eat grass, hay and other crops with nutrients in them. The nutrients from the food go into their milk. It takes a cow about two days to turn food into milk.

Like humans, cows only produce milk after having a baby. Dairy cows have one calf every year to keep up their supply of milk, which lasts for around 10 months after their baby is born.

CONTINUOUS PASTEURIZATION SYSTEM

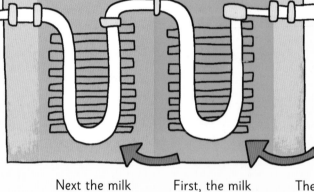

10

The cartons are collected by large refrigerated lorries and delivered to the shops nearby, ready to be bought by you and poured on your breakfast cereal!

Next the milk flows through a series of ice-cold metal plates, which instantly cool it.

First, the milk is pumped to a machine with a series of hot, thin metal plates. The milk flows along them for 30 minutes.

8

The raw milk is heated to kill any bacteria and then cooled. This is called pasteurization and makes the milk last longer.

9

The cooled, pasteurized milk is piped to the filling station, where a machine runs empty cartons along a conveyor belt, fills them with milk and stamps a heat-sealed lid on the top to prevent any bacteria from entering the carton.

Heating milk changes its taste. The temperature must be high for as little time as possible, but enough to kill bacteria. Most dairies produce 'high-temperature, short-time' (HTST) milk. It's heated to 72°C for 15 seconds. This gives the best taste and makes the milk last several days. Ultra-heat-treated (UHT) milk is heated to an 'ultra-high temperature'. It lasts for a long time, but tastes different than fresh milk.

2

The milk travels down into the cow's udders, which fill up. These need milking (emptying) around twice a day. It can be done by hand, but it is much quicker when done by machine. The cows are taken into the milking parlour. It's a large building with stalls – individual spaces for each cow to stand in.

It takes around 5 minutes to milk a cow. On some dairy farms, there are automated robotic milking stations. The cows are even automatically fed and scanned at the same time so the machine can monitor how much milk they are producing.

3 First, the cow's udders are checked to make sure they are clean. Then, a milking cluster is fixed to each of her four teats (nipples). The milking clusters copy the way a calf would suck for milk, which makes the cow release her milk and it flows from her udders into a hose.

4

The hoses from each stall lead into a big, refrigerated, stainless-steel tank. At this stage, the milk is called raw milk. To stop the fatty part (cream) from rising to the top, a long spoon called an agitator stirs it gently to keep it moving around.

Raw milk has some bacteria in it. This can be fine to drink if the milk is fresh, but if it is not kept cold, the bacteria multiply very quickly and the milk goes bad. Farmers have to do everything possible to keep the milk clean and cold, or they won't be able to sell the milk.

5

A milk tanker comes daily to collect the milk. The driver of the milk tanker is also a 'grader' and will taste and smell the milk for quality. If it seems fine, the driver takes a sample of the milk to test the bacteria levels. If the milk passes the test, it is pumped into a series of separate refrigerated compartments on the tanker. Each compartment is filled right to the top to stop the milk from sloshing round or mixing with air (which could have bacteria in it).

7

The milk is piped into a cold storage tank. The storage tank also has an agitator to make sure all the milk is kept at the same temperature and does not separate into cream. The dairy's laboratory takes samples of the milk, to again check the quality and levels of bacteria.

6

The tanker takes the milk to the dairy plant to be processed. When the milk arrives, it is pumped out through a meter. This measures how much milk there is, so the dairy plant knows how much to pay the farmer.

DAIRY PLANT

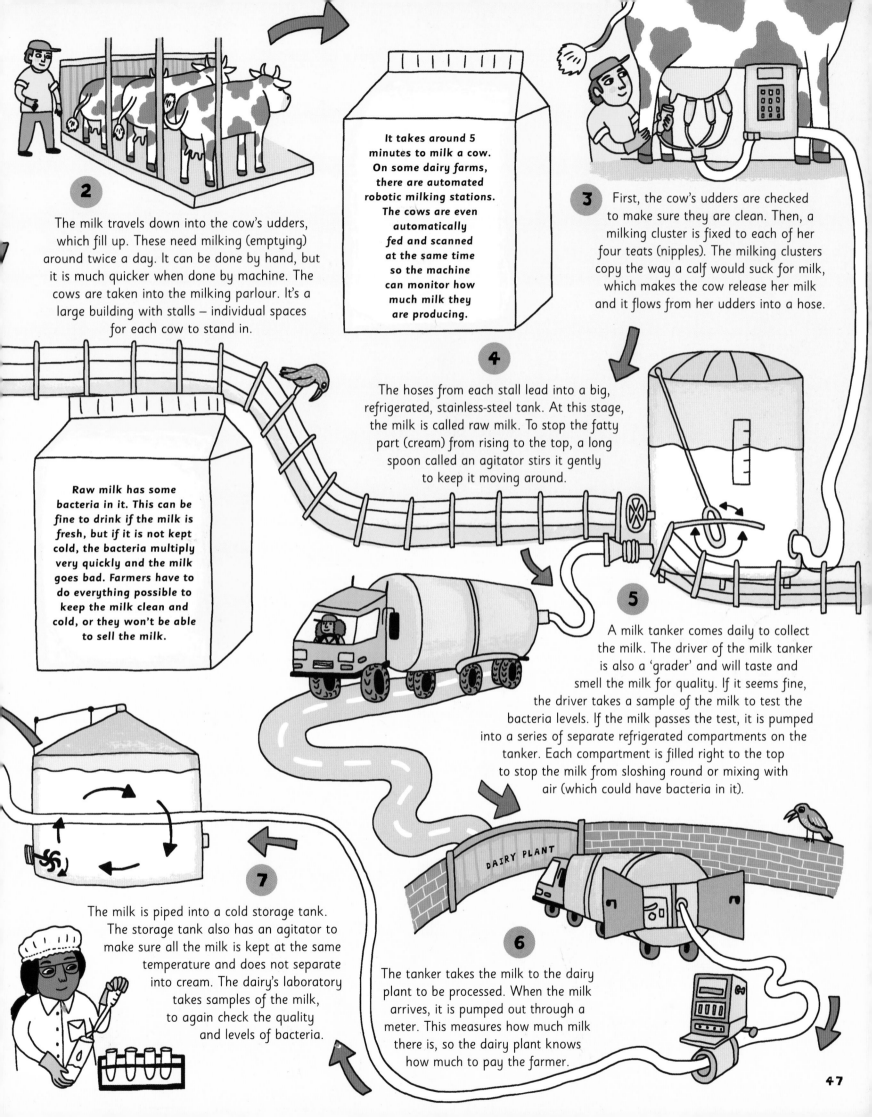

THE END

So, you've finished this book and come to the end of one journey.

Look around and try to notice the things you might take for granted. Think of all the machines, people, plants and processes that it takes just to make a bar of chocolate.

Imagine what it may take to blast an astronaut into space!